# ABOVE THE CEILING

By Tom Henry

While every precaution has been taken in the preparation of this book, the author and publisher assumes no responsibility for errors or omissions. Neither is any liability assumed from the use of the information contained herein.

Volume One - First Printing

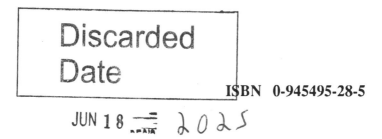

ISBN   0-945495-28-5

I would like to dedicate this book to my very dear friend Jerry Poulin 1934-1986. Much of this book is the humor that Jerry and I shared before his death. I trained Jerry as an industrial electrician in the mid 1960's and we shared many a laugh. I have felt his loss, but can always see his smile.

At the Democratic National Convention Memorial Service for his brother Jack in 1964, Bobby Kennedy recited a quotation from Shakespeare.

*" ...... when he shall die take him and cut him out in little stars and he will make the face of heaven so fine that all the world will be in love with night..."*

Do not stand at my grave and weep,
I am not there, I do not sleep.
I am a thousand winds that blow,
I am a diamond's glint on the snow.
I am the sunlight on ripened grain,
I am the gentle autumn rain.
When you awaken in the morning hush,
I am the swift, uplifting rush
of birds in circled flight,
I am the soft stars that shine at night.
Do not stand at my grave and cry.
I am not there.
I did not die.

Preface.

This is a book I've been requested to write by all of the electricians who have had to listen to my numerous "one-liners" over the years.

My qualifications to write a book on humor start at age eighteen when I started serving my apprenticeship under several Irish electricians on the railroad. How's that for a good start!

Then I went to work in the trenches digging ditches, running an air hammer, pushing a Georgia buggy, etc. with the common laborers. Then to the industry for nine years, then electrical construction, and later worked as an electrical inspector. Since then I have taught over 13,000 electricians. So I've picked up a few "one-liners" in my day.

I have always injected humor into my teaching. I have fun in my work. People listen better when they are smiling rather than frowning. Plus once you get people laughing you can tell them almost anything.

In this book I like to mess with the other guys; plumbers, inspectors, engineers, Republicans, etc. This book was not written to single out any one, in the "one-liners" you can substitute "Democrat" in place of Republican, "boss" in place of inspector, or "lawyer" in place of plumber if it makes you feel better.

I was always told that, a person that can't take a joke is most likely one. Always remember this, you don't stop laughing because you grow old; you grow old because you stop laughing.

I love to read books, I have always imagined that Paradise will be kind of a library. Any man that can surround himself with books will have at least one place in the world in which it will be possible to be happy.

In writing this book I tried to make it short and sweet. I have used not only "one-liners" but quotes from famous people, interesting questions, heavy thoughts to make you think, shocking facts, bumper stickers, etc.

I don't like a book that takes six pages just to say hello. I've always maintained in every fat book there is a thin book trying to get out. With some books the covers are too far apart!

Remember I'm not a joke writer, I just watch the Government and report the facts!

**This book is like a woman's skirt; long enough to cover the subject, but short enough to generate interest.**

We get letters..........

Thank you for sending me a copy of your new book. I'll waste no time reading it.

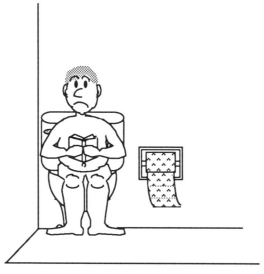

I am sitting here reviewing your new book which I have in front of me. Soon it will be behind me.

When visiting in the Orlando, Florida area after touring Walt Disney World, Sea World, Universal Studios, Cypress Gardens, Kennedy Space Center, etc. make it a point to visit **Mount Code** the highest point between the Appalachian Mountains and the 10,000 foot Haleakala Crater in the Haleakala National Park in Maui, Hawaii. Mount Code is 1283 feet higher than Mount Dora located 30 miles northwest of Orlando.

**MOUNT CODE**

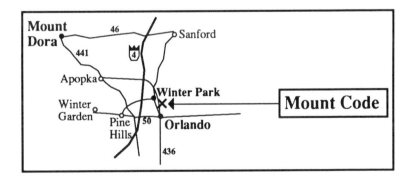

## For Your Information

If you have a favorite "one-liner" that you didn't see in this book write it down and send it to us. If your "one-liner" is used in the next edition of "Above The Ceiling" you will receive a free copy.

Send to:        Tom Henry's Code Electrical Classes Inc.
                6832 Hanging Moss Road
                Orlando, Florida   32807

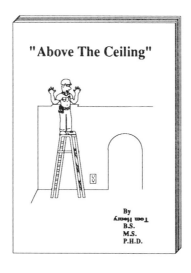

Cats are smarter than dogs. You can't get eight cats to pull a sled through snow.

The closest anyone ever comes to perfection is on a job application form.

My grandmother started walking five miles a day when she was sixty. She's ninety-two now, and we don't know where she is.

THE BUILDING WOULD BE MUCH
IMPROVED IF THEY SHOT
FEWER STUDS AND MORE
INSPECTORS.

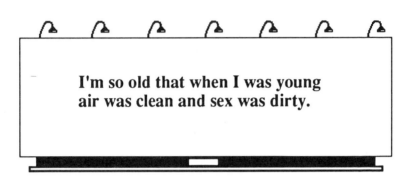

I'm so old that when I was young
air was clean and sex was dirty.

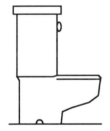

Only when the plumbing's
stopped up do you realize
that a flush is better than
a full house.

Americans are getting stronger.
Twenty-five years ago, it took two
adults to carry fifty dollars' worth of
groceries. Today, a child can do it.

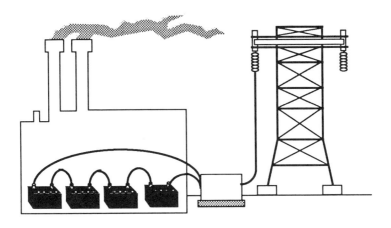

My hometown is so small they have four die-hard
batteries for the power supply!

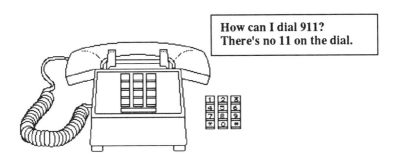

How can I dial 911?
There's no 11 on the dial.

# ELECTRICAL DESIGNING 1947

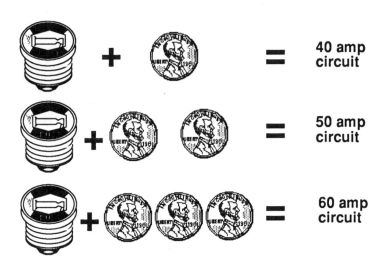

+ = 40 amp circuit

+ = 50 amp circuit

+ = 60 amp circuit

The real "chief" inspector.
(lots of feathers)

IT'S HARD TO BE AN ELECTRICIAN
UNLESS YOU HAVE THE
RIGHT CONNECTIONS!

# A Sharp Pain Between The Eyes

One day while at work Ralph developed a real sharp pain between his eyes which lasted all afternoon. At the dinner table Ralph mentioned the pain to his wife and she suggested seeing a doctor. After a careful examination the doctor explained to Ralph the only cure to relieve the pain is castration. Ralph screamed when told of the solution. Ralph said "no way am I going through with castration, why I'm still a young man. I'm only 41 years old. No way!"

The pain continued getting a little worse each day and three months later Ralph consented to the doctor to perform the operation as he couldn't stand the pain any longer.

Months after the surgery Ralph still couldn't seem to adjust to reality and chose to visit a psychiatrist. The psychiatrist told Ralph that he had been through a lot with the castration and that he needed to change his complete life style so he would feel better about himself. The doctor advised Ralph to buy a new home, new car and get a complete new wardrobe.

Ralph followed the doctor's advice and bought a new home and a new car. Then he went out to buy a new wardrobe. At the clothing store Ralph met a very interesting tailor. He was an elderly gentleman that had been fitting men for clothing for over 43 years. The tailor would look Ralph over and say "you wear a size 16 shirt". Ralph said you are exactly right. I have worn a size 16 for over twenty years. Next Ralph needed to pick out trousers and the tailor said "you wear a size 36-32 trouser". Exactly said Ralph.

Next was the choosing of socks when again the tailor was right about the size Ralph wore. Finally, Ralph said "this is amazing that you can just look at me and tell what size I wear without even measuring". The elderly tailor said "I should be able to, I've been doing this same job for 43 years".

The last item to pick out was underwear, the tailor said "you wear a size 36 shorts". Ralph said "well you finally got one wrong, I've worn a size 34 jockey shorts for over twenty years. You finally missed one".

The elderly tailor stated "I'm not wrong, you are wrong. You wear a size 36 and I don't have to measure you. SIZE 36 is what you need. You wear a size 34 and it will cause a sharp pain between your eyes"!

> Like dreams, small creeks sometimes grow into mighty rivers.

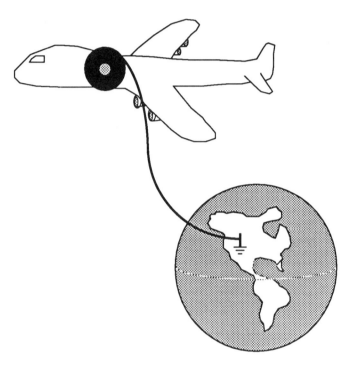

All I know is the inspector said all grounded circuits SHALL be connected to earth!

**HEAVY THOUGHTS:**

If your parents didn't have any children, it's most likely you won't either.

> He who expects nothing, ain't gonna be deceived.

The electrician had just finished installing the light when the inspector happened by. The inspector stated the installation was in violation and quoted section 225-26. It states electrical equipment shall not be installed on "live vegetation". The inspector stated the tree is "live vegetation".
The electrician said "that's not a tree, it's a pole, it just hasn't died yet!

HOROSCOPE - AQUARIUS  (Jan.20 - Feb.18)

You have an inventive mind and are inclined to be progressive. You lie a great deal. On the other hand you are inclined to be careless and impractical, causing you to make the same mistakes over and over again. People think you are stupid. The lights are on, but nobody is home.

**With the economy the way it is, we had to let mom go.**

It hurts when you're with me and when you're gone I wonder when you're coming back...
You're kind of like hemorroids.

One of the strongest characteristics of genius is the power of lighting its own fire.

The reason money doesn't grow on trees is that banks own all the branches.

The world is something that went from being flat, to being round, to being crooked.

Car sickness is what you get from looking at the sticker price.

**DARK SUCKER**

For years it has been believed that light bulbs give off light. Recently, scientists have proven just the opposite. Instead of a light bulb giving off light, they actually **suck dark.**

From now on light bulbs will be called "dark suckers". Scientists in the laboratory have proven that dark has a heavier mass than light and that dark is faster than light.

The dark sucker theory that light bulbs suck dark is based on an example such as the lamp in your living room. There is less dark close to the lamp than there is farther away from the lamp. The larger the dark sucker the lighter the living room.

Like other things, dark suckers don't last forever. Once they become full of dark, they can no longer suck. This is proven by the black spot on a dark sucker that is full.

The first dark sucker was a candle. A new candle has a white wick. As the candle is used the dark that is sucked up turns the wick black. The wick is a gauge to indicate the amount of dark that has been sucked up. If you held an object close to the wick of an operating candle the object would turn black because it got in the path of the dark flowing into the wick.

There are also portable dark suckers. The bulbs in a portable dark sucker cannot handle all of the dark by themselves, and must be aided by a dark storage unit. When the dark storage unit is full, it must be either emptied or replaced before the portable dark sucker can operate again.

Sucking dark creates heat, thus it is dangerous to touch a candle while it is sucking dark.

Dark is heavier than light. This is proven as one swims deeper, it gets darker and darker. This is because dark being heavier sinks to the bottom and light floats to the top.

Dark has advantages, we collect the dark that settles to the bottom of lakes and push it through turbines which generate electricity. We can route dark through rivers and streams and store huge amounts on the bottom of the ocean for future use.

**Dark suckers have changed our way of life!**

My grandmother is over eighty and still
doesn't need glasses.
Drinks right out of the bottle.

THE REASON MOST PEOPLE KEEP
CHANGING THEIR MINDS IS THAT
THEY NEVER FOUND ONE WORTH
KEEPING.

Today, the economy is truly electrical:
Everything is charged.

A spoonful of honey will
catch more flies than a
gallon of vinegar.

**Did you tell them to install a
big breaker this time?**

**Am I familar with raceways?
I've attended the Daytona 500
for 15 years.**

> If you can't go around it, over it or through it,
> you had better negotiate with it.

**Have you hugged your inspector today?**

AM    PM

**Even a broken watch is right twice a day.**

13

A man stranded alone on a deserted island for over seven years looked out to the ocean one day and saw a beautiful woman in a wet suit swimming towards the tiny island.

He rubbed his eyes in disbelief as he hadn't seen a person in over seven years, let alone a beautiful woman.

As he introduced himself he told her the story of how he wound up stranded alone on this tiny island over seven years ago. She said "you've been alone for seven years, I bet you'd like to have a cigarette". He said "I'd love to. You don't mean to tell me you've got cigarettes with you"? She unzipped a pocket on the right arm of her wet suit and pulled out a pack of cigarettes and they both lit up.

She said "seven years alone on this island, I bet you'd like to have a cocktail". "A cocktail!" he said. "You don't mean to tell me you've got booze with you"? She unzipped a pocket on the left arm of her wet suit and pulled out a flask and they both had a drink.

As they sat on the beach smoking their cigarettes, drinking and chatting, she took a hold of the zipper at the top of her wet suit and unzipped it all the way down past her navel and looked at him with her beautiful dreamy eyes and said "would you like to play around"?

He said "you don't mean to tell me you got a set of golf clubs in there too"!

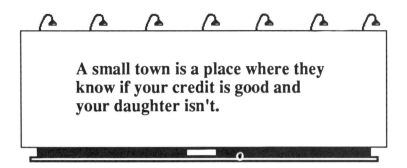

A small town is a place where they know if your credit is good and your daughter isn't.

LIFE IS LIKE A SHOWER: A WRONG TURN CAN LEAVE YOU IN HOT WATER.

You know the world's in trouble when it takes 5,000 laws to enforce the Ten Commandments.

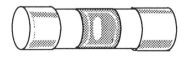

People who constantly blow a fuse are usually in the dark.

I discovered how to hammer nails without hitting my thumb. Let someone else hold the nail.

Measure twice, cut once.

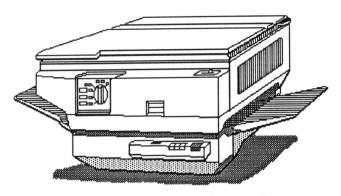

Machines should work; people should think.

YOU CAN'T FALL OFF THE FLOOR.

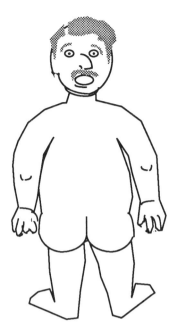

**Well, at least I got my head screwed on right!**

## SMOKERS GO TO HEAVEN, SOONER.

When I was a boy of fourteen, my father was so ignorant I could hardly stand to have the old man around. But when I got to be twenty-one, I was amazed to see how much he had learned in seven years.

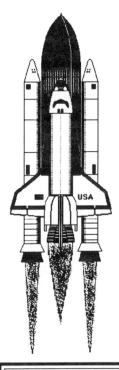

One electrician said to another "we
should volunteer to go to the moon".
The other electrician asked why?
The first one replied "I read where
your sex urge is 8 times greater".
His wife overheard him and quickly
replied "don't waste your time
honey, 8 times zero is still zero".

What lies behind you and what lies before
you are tiny matters compared
to what lies within you.

## ELECTRICAL PIONEERS

| Benjamin Franklin | Thomas Edison | Andre Ampere | Willard Watt | Tom Transformer |

**Read this sentence:**

> FEDERAL FUSES ARE THE RE-
> SULT OF YEARS OF SCIENTIF-
> IC STUDY COMBINED WITH THE
> EXPERIENCE OF YEARS.

Now read it once more, and count
the F's in the sentence. How many
did you find?
(see answer section of book)

---

Aerodynamically the bumble bee shouldn't be
able to fly, but the bumble bee doesn't know it,
so it goes on flying anyway.

---

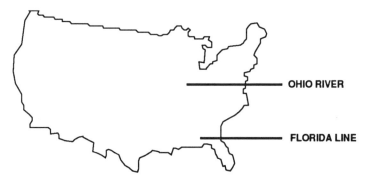

OHIO RIVER

FLORIDA LINE

When arriving at the Florida state line the Welcome Center provides the traveler with a glass of orange juice.

When arriving at the Ohio River traveling north they should give you a shot of penicillin.

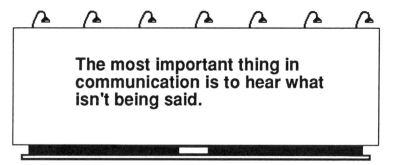

The most important thing in communication is to hear what isn't being said.

Mondays are the potholes in the road of life.

EVERYWHERE IS WITHIN WALKING DISTANCE IF YOU HAVE THE TIME.

> Genius is 3% inspiration and 97% perspiration.

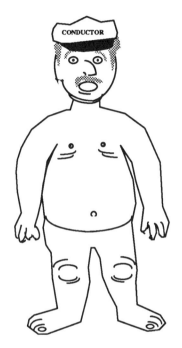

## A BARE CONDUCTOR.

When angry, count to four;
when very angry,
swear.

## HEAVY THOUGHTS:

Late one night three electricians arrived in a
small town to stay overnight and start a job the
next morning. The town only had one motel
which only had one room left that was vacant.
The cost of the room was $30 so each
electrician paid $10 to split the room cost
three ways.
Later the bellboy knocked on the door to
inform them there had been a mistake in the
room charge. The cost of the room was only
$25 and not $30 so they had a refund coming
of $5. One electrician decided with the $5 to
tip the bellboy $2 and divide the remaining $3
evenly among them. But another electrician
couldn't figure the calculation and said "wait a
minute, three of us put in $10 each and
received $1 back, that means each of us paid
$9 for the room". 3 electricians X $9 = $27
plus the $2 tip to the bellboy = $29.

**WHERE'S THE OTHER DOLLAR???**

Anyone can
steer the ship
when the sea is
calm.

22

My wife deserves the credit, she made me a millionaire, before the divorce I had two million.

 Paying alimony is the equivalent of having the TV on after you've fallen asleep.

SINCE I'VE GIVEN UP HOPE, I FEEL MUCH BETTER.

Alimony is like buying oats for a dead horse.

HOROSCOPE - ARIES (March 21 - April 19)

You are the pioneer type and hold people in contempt. You are quick tempered, impatient and scornful of advice. You are basically lazy and have always depended on someone else (meal ticket). You are not very nice. You are needed, like a fish needs a bicycle.

**Nan Linear**

**Carl Conduit**

**Bob Bulb**

**Wayne Wire**

**Vic Volt**

**Ruth Resistor**

**Millie Amp**

**Mike Roy Amp**

**Buddy Nobuddy**

Never argue with a fool.
People might not know the difference.

There was a time when the only little black book that belonged to a clergyman was the Bible.

**A LEADING AUTHORITY IS ANYONE WHO HAS GUESSED RIGHT MORE THAN ONCE.**

In the race for quality there is no finish line.

It use to be a contractor was giving jobs away to keep the employees on the payroll. The economy is so bad now the contractor is buying jobs.

# The New York Times

## AC - DC will be at Madison Square Garden tonight!

**LOCALS STUNNED**

**TORONTO, ATHENS, LONDON, PARIS, ROME MOSCOW, WASHINGTON**

TRENDS

**GENEVA SHOCKED**

**NO PROBLEM!**

**CHICAGO**

**SEATTLE**

**SAN FRANCISCO**

**HOUSTON**

If you've never seen AC or DC here is your chance.

26

## HOW ELECTRICITY WAS DISCOVERED
### the TALE of the TAIL

Have you ever wondered why Ben Franklin was flying his kite in a violent thunder storm? Most people fly their kite on a clear, windy day; not in pouring rain.

As the tale of "the tail" is told:
In the year of 1752, in an alley near his home in Philadelphia, Ben was running up and down the alley trying to get his kite up in the air.

His wife observed him running up and down the alley, from the kitchen window. She lifted the window and hollered at the top of her voice "Ben, what in the world are you doing running up and down the alley in a lightning storm and pouring rain?"

Ben replied, "I'm trying to get my kite up in the air!"
She answered, "You'll never get it up without a little tail."
Ben replied, "That's what I said this morning and you told me to go fly a kite!"

## AN ELECTRICIAN QUALIFIED TO REMOVE YOUR SHORTS!

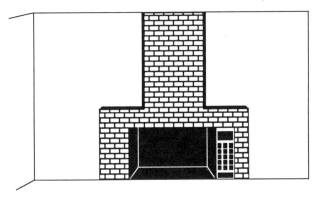

Microwave Fireplace: 3 hours of entertainment in 6 minutes.

28

> The great calamity is not to have failed but to have failed to try.

**3rd HARMONIC**

> If you build a better mousetrap, you will catch better mice.

# DESCENDANTS of ELECTRICAL PIONEERS

**Mary Magnetic**

**Harry Harmonic**

**Greg Ground**

**Frank Filament**

**Wanda Wye**

**Eric Electron**

**Ron Relay**

**Tim Terminal**

**Cathy Coil**

> He is only exempt from failures who makes no efforts.

When I was young I was so broke once I forgot whether you cut steak with a knife or drank it with a spoon.

A wedding is a funeral where you can smell your own flowers.

HOROSCOPE - CANCER  (June 21 - July 22)

You are sympathetic and understanding to other peoples problems. They think you are a sucker. You are always putting things off. That's why you'll never make anything of yourself. Most welfare recipients are Cancer people.

**I never think of the future.
It comes soon enough.**

Heaven goes by
favor; if it went
by merit, you
would stay out
and your dog
would go in.

He who waits for a dead man's shoes
may long go barefoot.

If you ever need a helping hand you'll
find one at the end of your arm.

> A man can fail many times but he isn't a failure until he begins to blame somebody else.

ASH ELECTRICAL

Employment Services

I realize that I'm over qualified, but I promise to use only half of my ability.

## THE PROBLEM WITH JUMPIMG TO CONCLUSIONS IS THAT THERE'S NEVER A SAFETY NET.

### HOROSCOPE - LEO (July 23 - Aug.22)

You consider youself a born leader. You are a legend, in your own mind. Others think you are pushy. Most Leo people are bullies. You are vain and dislike honest criticism. Your arrogance is disgusting. Leo people are known thieves.

**Did you know?**

Birds take advantage of Earth's magnetic field in their seasonal migrations. A very small magnetic crystal located between the brain and the skull strongly suggests that birds use the geomagnetic field for orientation.

---

The boss is such a perfectionist, if he was married to Raquel Welch, he'd even expect her to cook.

**7th HARMONIC**

**Alcohol is what makes married men see double and feel single.**

**I distrust camels, and anyone else who can go a week without a drink**

**Did you know?**

**That "romex" can only be used in buildings up to three floors. Do you know why "romex" can't be used on the 4th floor?**

**Answer: For safety, the ladder on the fire truck will only reach up to 3 floors.**

**HOROSCOPE - VIRGO (Aug.23 - Sept.22)**

**You are the logical type and hate disorder. This nit-picking is sickening to your friends. You are cold and unemotional and sometimes fall asleep while making love. Virgos make good bus drivers.**

A lady calls the fire department to report that a man is on a ladder and trying to get into her second floor bedroom window. The fireman replies, "this is the fire department, you need to call the police department". The lady says "no I want the fire department because he needs a longer ladder"!

| S | M | T | W | T | F | S |
|---|---|---|---|---|---|---|
| 1 | 2 | 3 | 4 | 5 | 6 | 7 |
| 8 | 9 | 10 | 11 | 12 | 13 | 14 |
| 15 | 16 | 17 | 18 | 19 | 20 | 21 |
| 22 | 23 | 24 | 25 | 26 | 27 | 28 |
| 29 | 30 | 31 | | | | |

My doctor gave me three weeks to live. I hope they're in September.

**You can't do it.**

**THINK POSITIVE,
I CONDUIT!**

He's so slow it takes him an
hour and a half to watch 60 minutes.

Did you know?

Over one million drill motors
were sold last year. But, no
one wanted a drill, what they
wanted was a hole!

TO A PLUMBER,
SIX BOWLING SHIRTS ARE
CONSIDERED A GREAT WARDROBE.

I SPENT MOST OF MY MONEY
ON WOMEN AND BEER,
THE REST I JUST WASTED.

There are three kinds of people:

Those who make things happen.
Those who watch things happen.
Those who wonder what happened.

**JUNIOR INSPECTOR**
(one feather)

The man who believes he can do something is probably right, and so is the man who believes he can't.

Education consists mainly in what we have unlearned.

**HEAVY THOUGHTS:**

Very few people realize that I was one of a set of twins. The nurse accidentally drowned one of us in the bath tub, but no one could tell which one. Everyone thought that I was the one that lived, but I wasn't. It was my brother who lived and I was the one that drowned.

# OHM SWEET OHM!

Have you ever experienced a case of a rodent or squirrel becoming entangled with a transformer and causing a fire?
Have you ever wondered how birds can sit on electric wires without electrocuting themselves? Do you know why they don't get electrocuted?

See answer section of this book.

> **Every job is a self-portrait of the person who did it.**

**Remember I am an inspector.
"Sir, I will respect your secret".**

> The secret of success in life is for a person to be ready when his opportunity comes.

The only man who makes money following the races is one who does it with a broom and shovel.

**Did you know?**

The laser can destroy a bulldozer over 2000 yards away, but yet this same laser can be used for delicate surgery to the human eye.

Just remember, to turn the power switch from bulldozer to eyeball!

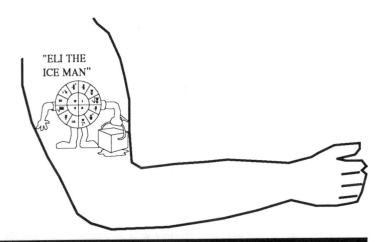

"ELI THE ICE MAN"

**HOROSCOPE - SAGITTARIOUS  (Nov.22 - Dec.21)**

You are optimistic and enthusiastic. You have a reckless tendency to rely on luck since you lack talent. The majority of Sagittarians are drunks or dope fiends. Sagittarians have trouble with doing two things at once, like walking while chewing gum.

It takes both rain and sunshine to make a rainbow.

"I will study and get ready and some day my chance will come"

Experience ...
is simply the name we give our mistakes.

My grandfather lives in a town so small he always mailed his utility payment addressed simply: THE ELECTRIC COMPANY. Well, last month the new postmaster returned it stamped: INSUFFICIENT ADDRESS. Grandpa promptly remailed it with his own message scribbled across the envelope: IT'S NEXT TO THE DAMN POST OFFICE!

No one can make you feel more humble than an electrician who discovers you've been trying to wire something yourself.

HAPPINESS CAN BE FOUND UNDER "H" IN THE DICTIONARY

ALL PROGRESS HAS RESULTED FROM THOSE WHO TOOK UNPOPULAR POSITIONS.

HOROSCOPE - CAPRICORN (Dec.22 - Jan.19)

You are conservative and afraid of taking risks. You don't do much of anything and are lazy. There has never been a Capricorn of any importance. Capricorns should avoid standing still too long, as they tend to take root and become trees. A Capricorn makes a room brighter by leaving.

> Money won't buy happiness, but it will help you search for it more comfortably.

Did you know?

Training is everything.

The peach was once a bitter almond; cauliflower is nothing but cabbage with a college education!

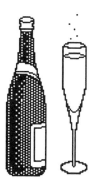

I drink too much. Last time I gave a urine sample there was an olive in it.

Common sense is instinct, and enough of it is genius.

**QUESTION?**

What two questions can never
be answered with a yes?

See answer section.

**"Nuisance Tripping"**

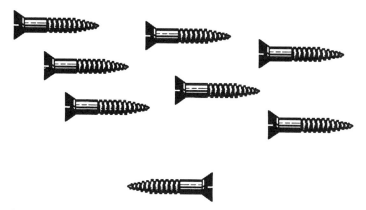

As an electrician was observing his helper inserting screws he noticed that every once in a while the helper would pull a screw from his pocket, look at it and then throw it on the floor and reach in his pocket and get another screw, look at it and insert it. The electrician asked "why every once in a while are you throwing the screw on the floor"? The helper replied "the head is on the wrong end!"

---

**Obstacles are what you see when you take your eyes off the goal.**

---

**Laziness travels so slowly that poverty soon overtakes him.**

WHATEVER HITS
THE FAN, MAY NOT
BE EVENLY DISTRIBUTED

I'M NOT BALD, THAT'S A SOLAR
COLLECTOR FOR A
SEX MACHINE!

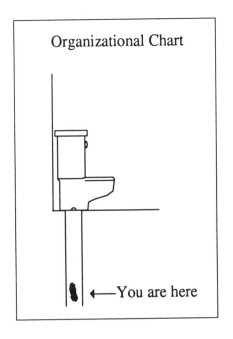

Organizational Chart

←You are here

Father walking along with his son, the son asks his father, "does lightning affect the direction of raindrops in a storm?"
"I don't know," answered the father.
The son asks his father, "is a lightning bolt hotter than the sun?"
"I don't know," answered the father.
The son asks his father, "how many volts are in a lightning bolt?"
"I don't know," answered the father.
"Father, I hope I'm not bothering you by asking you all these questions," replied the son.
"No problem," said the father. "How are you ever going learn if you don't ask questions?"

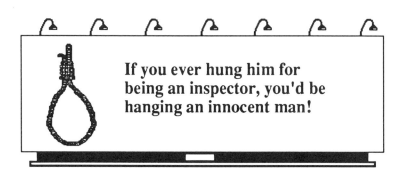

If you ever hung him for being an inspector, you'd be hanging an innocent man!

Those with the most horse sense do the least kicking.

  On a flight an electrician kept pushing the flight attendant button instead of the reading light button.

The flight attendant said "if you can't tell the difference between a light bulb and a stewardess, someday you're in for a real shock"!

# Excuses are the nails to build a house of failure.

## A REAL WIRE NUT!

# GRANDCHILDREN of ELECTRICAL PIONEERS

PAUL PIPE

TWILA TAPE

DICK DELTA

FREDA FUSE

BILL BAKELITE

CONNIE CODE

GENE GENERATOR

MARGARET MOTOR

BONNIE BOX

NANCY NEUTRAL

RALPH RECEPTACLE

LAURA LIGHT

51

A minister dies and goes to heaven, where he finds a long line at St. Peter's gate. The minister rushes to the front of the line and explains to St. Peter all the years he has faithfully served the Lord and he shouldn't have to wait in line. While he's explaining an electrician rushes to the front of the line, waves to St. Peter and walks immediately through the Pearly Gates. "Hey!" The minister shouts. "How come you let an electrician through ahead of me?" "Oh," says St. Peter, "That's God. Sometimes he likes to play electrician."

Recession is so bad, even the accounts that don't intend to pay ain't buying.

Don't force it; get a larger hammer.

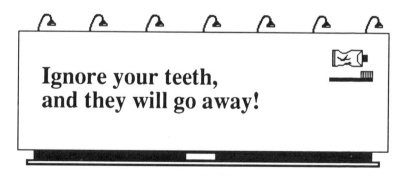

Ignore your teeth,
and they will go away!

You got your degree at Penn State and I got mine at the State Pen.

---

Time never waits for a better day.
Do it now.

---

I had plastic surgery last week.
I cut up my credit cards.

---

WIRING IS NO HOBBY,
HAVE YOUR ELECTRICAL WORK
INSPECTED!

> Children certainly brighten up a home, did you ever see one remember to turn off a light?

For three days after death hair and fingernails continue to grow but the phone calls taper off.

When the subject becomes totally obsolete we make it a required subject.

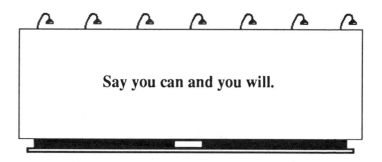

Say you can and you will.

# THE STATION

Tucked away in our subconscious minds is an idyllic vision. We see ourselves on a long, long trip that almost spans the continent. We're traveling by passenger train and out the windows we drink in the passing scene of cars on nearby highways, of children waving at a crossing, of cattle grazing on a distant hillside, of smoke pouring from a power plant, of row upon row of corn and wheat, of flatlands and valleys, of mountains and rolling hillsides, of city skylines and village halls, of biting winter and blazing summer and cavorting spring and docile fall.

But uppermost in our minds is the final destination. On a certain day at a certain hour we will pull into the station. There will be bands playing and flags waving. And once we get there so many wonderful dreams will come true. So many wishes will be fulfilled and so many pieces of our lives finally will be neatly fitted together like a completed jigsaw puzzle. How restlessly we pace the aisles, damning the minutes for loitering ... waiting, waiting, waiting for the station.

However, sooner or later we must realize there is no one station, no one place to arrive once and for all. The true joy of life is the trip. The station is only a dream. It constantly outdistances us.

"When we reach the station, that will be it" we cry. Translated it means, "when I'm 18, that will be it! When I buy a new 450 SL Mercedes Benz, that will be it! When I put the last kid through college, that will be it! When I have paid off the mortgage, that will be it! When I win a promotion, that will be it! When I reach the age of retirement, that will be it! I shall live happily ever after!"

Unfortunately, once we get "it", then "it" disappears. The station somehow hides itself at the end of an endless track.

"Relish the moment" is a good motto, especially when coupled with Psalm 118:24: "This is the day which the Lord hath made, we will rejoice and be glad in it." It isn't the burdens of today that drive men mad. Rather, it is the regret over yesterday or fear of tomorrow. Regret and fear are twin thieves who rob us of today.

So stop pacing the aisles and counting the miles. Instead, climb more mountains, eat more ice cream, go barefoot oftener, swim more rivers, watch more sunsets, laugh more and cry less. Life must be lived as we go along. The station will come soon enough.

> We can do anything we want if we stick to it long enough.

**Which is the correct way to install toilet paper?**

(see answer section)

> A conservative is a man with two perfectly good legs, who has never learned to walk.

**I'm saving electricity, so I plug my clock in only when I want to know what time it is.**

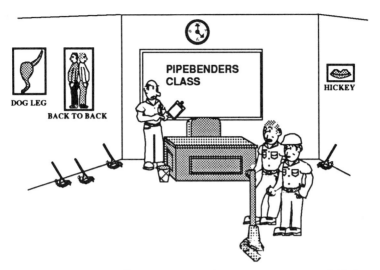

DOG LEG

BACK TO BACK

PIPEBENDERS CLASS

HICKEY

Do you know how to make a saddle?

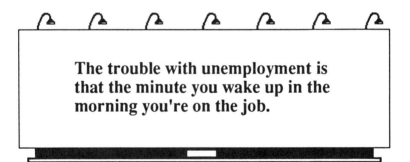

The trouble with unemployment is that the minute you wake up in the morning you're on the job.

What is the one thing that many beautiful women have guaranteed to knock your eyes out?

(see answer section)

## ELECTRICITY IS DELIVERED FRESH!

Electric current travels 186,000 miles per second. Which means when you turn the light switch on, current can flow from New York to Honolulu and back over 18 times in one second.

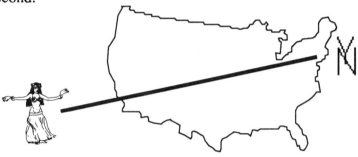

At the close of the seminar the speaker asked the group if he had succeeded in making himself clear. One person stood up and said, "yes, sir, except one part during which you stood between me and the chalk board." The speaker replied, "well, I did my best to make myself clear but evidently could not make myself transparent."

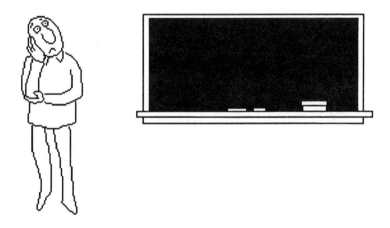

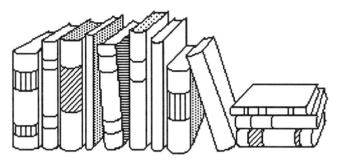

Never lend books, for no one ever returns them. The only books I have in my library are those that other people have lent me.

Confidence is the thing you had before you knew better.

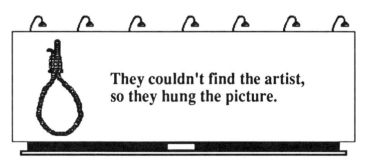

They couldn't find the artist, so they hung the picture.

If your time ain't come not even a doctor can kill you.

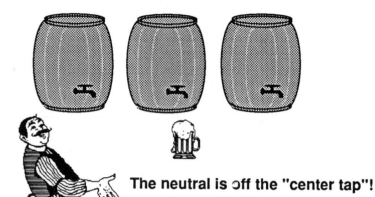

The neutral is off the "center tap"!

LEFTOVER NUTS NEVER MATCH
LEFTOVER BOLTS.

I've decided to give you a little pay raise, but
please promise not to tell the other workers.
Don't worry about me telling anyone boss,
I'm just as embarrassed about it as you are!

**CONTRARY TO POPULAR BELIEF THIS TOILET DOES NOT CONTAIN RARE TROPICAL GOLDFISH.**

**YOU MAY FLUSH IT!**

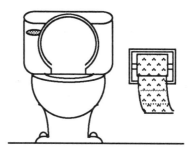

**I'm prepared to go anywhere, as long as it is forward.**

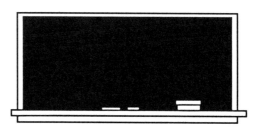

Bored with the seminar speaker the electrician raised his hand and said "excuse me, my leg has gone to sleep. Do you mind if I join it?"

## SHOCKING BUT TRUE

Georg Simon Ohm came from a
long line of locksmiths in Germany,
but he decided to become a
scientist instead. He became a
professor of mathematics and of
physics, and in 1827 he published
what is now known as Ohm's Law,
a basic law of electricity. Ohm,
who was born in 1787 and died in
1854, wasn't particularly
well-regarded in his day, but
eventually others agreed that his
theories were right, and today his
name lives on in two words. The
ohm is a unit of electrical
resistance; the mho, which is
pronounced moe and is ohm
spelled backward, is a unit of
conductance that is reciprocal to
the ohm.

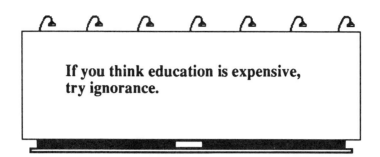

**If you think education is expensive, try ignorance.**

**The more I ask of myself, the more I find I have to give.**

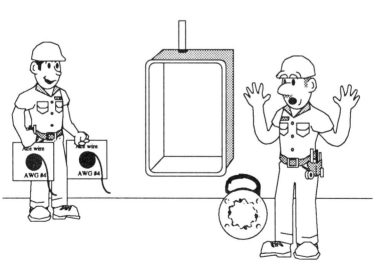

The supply house didn't have any #8 wire, so I got two boxes of #4 wire..... Okay?

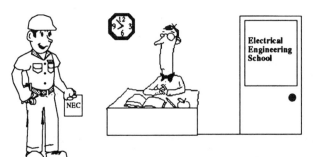

So you have completed a 4-year apprenticeship as a journeyman electrician, worked as a helper for 3 years, worked at an electrical supply company 2 summers part-time, worked as an industrial electrician for 6 years, worked as a residential-commercial master electrician 3 years designing services, working with the inspectors, plans examiners, and building departments pulling permits. Have owned your own electrical business for 3 years, bidding, estimating, supervising, etc.......
And now you've decided you want to be an electrical engineer.

With your electrical background, in order for you to qualify to enter the engineering school you are facing the biggest obstacle of your career, you will have to have half of your brain surgically removed!

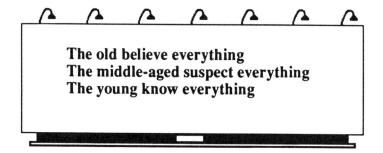

The old believe everything
The middle-aged suspect everything
The young know everything

# THEY HAVE AN ALL-ELECTRIC HOME, EVEN THE CHAIRS.

Honest, I don't know why the meter reading is lower this month!

65

BREAKFAST SPECIAL
TWO EGGS, GRITS,
HOME FRIES, TOAST

Menu

How do you like your eggs?
I really like my eggs!
I like 'em a lot!

Happiness is found along the way,
not at the end of the road.

IF I HAD KNOWN I WAS GONNA
LIVE THIS LONG,
I WOULD HAVE TOOK BETTER
CARE OF MYSELF!

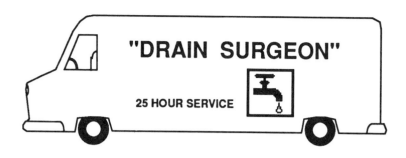

The sophisticated plumber.

Electrical, no bull....

Where you come from is not nearly as
important as where you are going.

**If you don't think women are explosive, try dropping one.**

**The only time the boss know's what he's doing!**

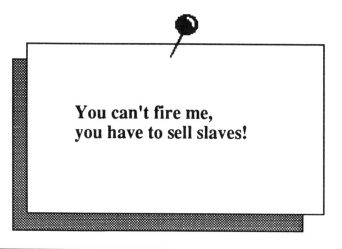

You can't fire me,
you have to sell slaves!

Give to the world the best you have and
the best will come back to you.

**I DON'T HAVE ULCERS,
I GIVE THEM!**

KEEP OUT

$\Omega$

DANGER
ONE
MILLION
OHMS

## SHOCKING BUT TRUE

Andre Marie Ampere was conducting experiments in France at the same time Ohm was working in Germany. Ampere, who lived from 1775 to 1836, more or less developed the science of electromagnetism, and today his name lives on in the lower-case-a ampere, a unit of electric current that is sometimes known as an amp. (Ampere led an unhappy life. When Andre was 18, his father was guillotined in the Reign of Terror, a tragedy that threw the youth into shock; he didn't read or speak for the next year and spent most of his days lying down and looking at the sky.)

**There is no way to find out why a snorer can't hear himself snore.**

# Why does electricity shock people?

# (see answer section)

Some people are electrifying - they light up a room when they leave.

Buy American
and save
a job
...in Mexico

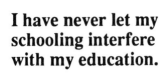

I have never let my
schooling interfere
with my education.

I shall make electricity so cheap that
only the rich can afford to burn candles.

This is the machine age. The only thing
people do by hand is pick their nose.

## Insulated Conductor

The brain is a wonderful organ. It starts working the moment you get up in the morning, and does not stop until you get into the office.

## SHOCKING BUT TRUE

While Ohm worked in Germany
and Ampere in France, Alessandro
Giuseppe Anastasio Volta was
experimenting in Italy. Volta, who
was raised as one of nine children
in a very poor but noble family,
became one of the greatest
scientists of his time and a
personal favorite of Napoleon,
who eventually made him Count
Volta. Volta died in 1827, at age
82, but his name lives on today in
the word volt, a unit of electric
potential and electromotive force.

**Law of Hydrodynamics:
When the body is
immersed in water,
the telephone rings.**

**A secretary must think like a man,
act like a lady,
look like a girl -
and work like a dog.**

If you would not be forgotten as soon as you
are dead, either write things worth reading or
do things worth writing.

The difficult we do
immediately, the impossible
takes a little longer.

## SHOCKING BUT TRUE

In Scotland, James Watt was messing around with steam, and in the 1790's he developed the first true steam engine. He spent most of his life perfecting it - though he paused now and then to invent other things, including a clothes dryer - and in his honor the International Electrical Conference gave the name watt to a unit of electrical power. Watt died in 1819 at age 83.

There are those who understand everything till one puts it into words.

A secret is something you tell only one person at a time.

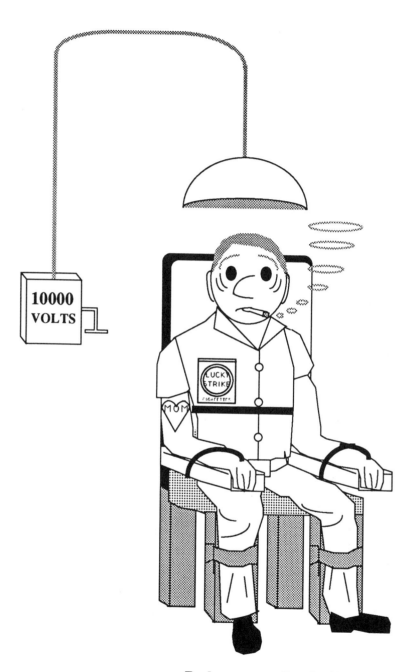

**Be happy, go Lucky!!!**

# SHOCKING BUT TRUE

Nikola Tesla 1856-1943. In his second year at Polytechnic Institute, Nikola, an immigrant from Yugoslavia, asked his professor whether the excessive sparking at the brushes could be eliminated. His professor ridiculed his idea and embarrassed him in front of his fellow students. Later while working at the Edison Machine Works in New Jersey, he tried to interest his employer in his new induction motor and his ideas on AC. Thomas Edison would hear none of it. Three years later, Tesla established his own laboratory in New York and developed his motor system. This was the first synchronous motor. Telsa went on to develop the complete polyphase system. The split-phase motor and a standard 60 cycle frequency also belong to him. Telsa died without realizing his dream, but his genius led the way into a new world of generating, transmitting, and using electric power.

"I'm going to give you something to help you sleep... take this Code Book..."

I went on a diet, swore off drinking and heavy eating, and in fourteen days I lost two weeks.

Why travel, I'm already there!

Winter Park, Florida

Everything comes to him who waits,
except a loaned book.

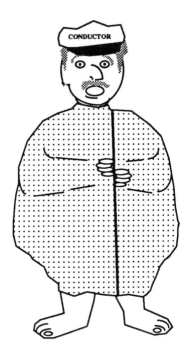

## Covered Conductor

Bad breath is better than no
breath at all!

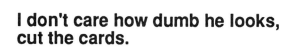

I don't care how dumb he looks,
cut the cards.

If I were your wife, I would
poison your soup. Ma'am if I
were your husband, I would
drink it!

If the working man gets his hours reduced
much more he will be in danger of
meeting himself coming home every
time he goes to work.

Do it tomorrow. You've made
enough mistakes for one day.

The wages of sin are high -
but get your money's worth.

Edison did not invent the first
talking machine. He invented the
first one that could be turned off.

The difference between the
right word and almost the
right word is the difference
between lightning and the
lightning bug.

Your ability to get to the bottom of things will be noted.

Amuse the reader at the same time that you
instruct him.

I've read so much about the bad
effects of drinking, smoking and sex.
I've decided to give up ............
reading!

We consume our tomorrows fretting about
our yesterdays.

> I'm a great believer in luck and I find the
> harder I work the more I have of it.

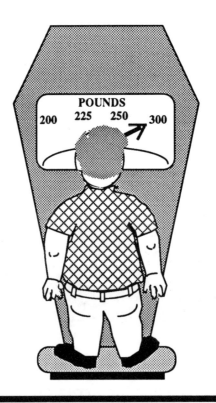

**Fortune Card**

**COME BACK WHEN**
**YOU'RE ALONE!**

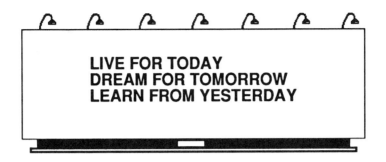

**LIVE FOR TODAY**
**DREAM FOR TOMORROW**
**LEARN FROM YESTERDAY**

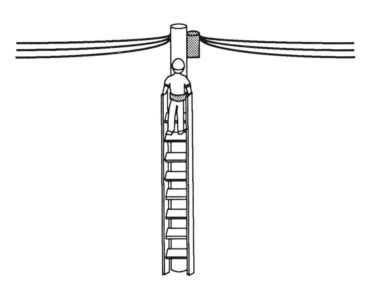

Today you will have an opportunity to rise above it all!

Good judgement comes from experience; and experience, well, that comes from bad judgement.

## SHOCKING BUT TRUE

An elderly gentleman received an
electric razor as a Christmas gift from
his wife. The problem was the house
was over 100 years old and did not
have a receptacle in the bathroom to
plug the razor into. All the bathroom
had was a ceiling light with a wall
switch.
So they called an electrician to install
a receptacle in the bathroom.
The electrician being very
knowlegeable of the Code installed a
GFCI duplex receptacle.
When finished he called the gentleman
in the bathroom so he could try out his
new razor. It worked just fine. The
electrician handed him the bill and
starting packing up his tools. The
elderly gentleman said "wait a minute,
you installed the GFCI receptacle
where my ceiling light switch was, now
I don't have any switch to turn my
ceiling light on or off".
The electrician reached over to the
GFCI receptacle and pushed "test,
"reset", "test", "reset" and the ceiling
light went on and off!

**"I gave her a ring, and she gave me the finger."**

An electrician went to Las Vegas to gamble driving an $82,000 Mercedes. After three days of gambling he went home in a brand new $500,000 bus!

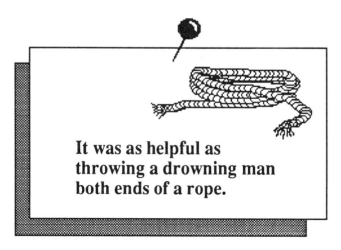

It was as helpful as throwing a drowning man both ends of a rope.

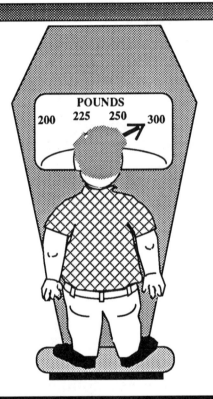

**If nobody dropped out at the eighth grade, who would hire the college graduates?**

POUNDS

200    225    250    300

Fortune Card

ONE AT A TIME
PLEASE!

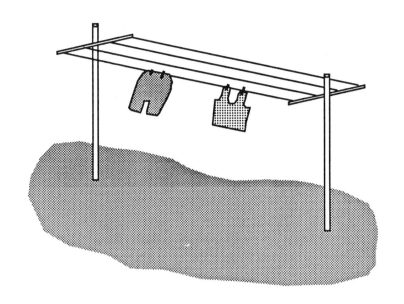

## A 2-pole 4-wire dryer!

If you want your dreams to come true,
don't sleep.

EGO IS THE FALLACY
WHEREBY A GOOSE
THINKS HE'S A SWAN.

A contract is where the large print
giveth and the small print taketh away.

Death sneaks up on you like a
windshield sneaks up on a bug.

The contractor that works for nothing,
is always busy.

There is hardly anything in
the world that some man
cannot make a little worse,
and sell a little cheaper.

A conference is a gathering of important people who singly can do nothing but together can decide that nothing can be done.

A single conversation with a wise man is better than ten years of study.

His problem is that it takes him six weeks to read the Book of the Month.

I can live for two months on a good compliment.

**The only reason some people get lost in thought is because it's unfamiliar territory.**

"This is your power day."

I DRINK TO MAKE OTHER PEOPLE MORE INTERESTING.

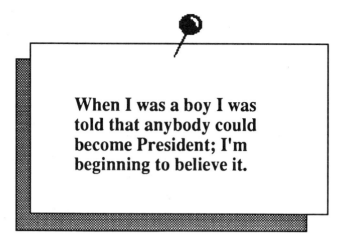

When I was a boy I was told that anybody could become President; I'm beginning to believe it.

The mistakes are all there waiting to be made.

ON | OFF

**In any electrical circuit, appliances and wiring will burn out to protect the circuit breaker.**

 A race horse is an animal that can take thousands of people for a ride at the same time.

**FRIENDS DON'T LET THEIR FRIENDS BECOME INSPECTORS.**

> I may have my faults,
> but being wrong ain't one of them.

$$4 \ (wr)^2 / 000002 - 32 = R4$$

Yes, I know that Ralph.... everybody knows that
two wrongs don't make a right! But look: Four
wrongs squared, divided by two wrongs to the
sixth power, minus 32, do make a right!

> **A BATHING BEAUTY IS SOMEONE
> WORTH WADING FOR.**

We don't know a millionth of
one percent about anything.

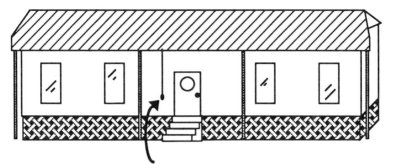

**First Canopy Switch**

HEAVY THOUGHTS:

I can't believe I forgot
to have children.

I almost got a girl pregnant
in high school. It's costing me
a fortune to keep the rabbit
on a life-support system.

95

**FORBES LIST OF THE RICHEST PEOPLE IN AMERICA.**

Every morning I get up and look through the Forbes list of the richest people in America. If I'm not there, I go to work.

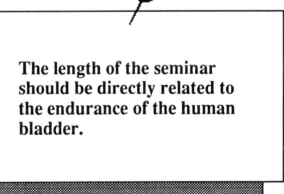

The length of the seminar should be directly related to the endurance of the human bladder.

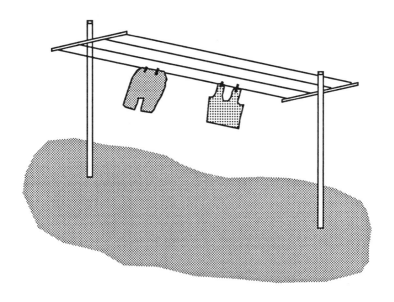

## Solar clothes dryer.

When I feel athletic, I go to a sports bar.

## The Ghost Story

When Ralph was a young boy he collected everything that had a ghost on it; key chains, comic books, Halloween decorations, etc. He read and studied everything ever written about ghosts. Later in life Ralph decided to write a book on all his experiences and studies of ghosts. The book became a big seller and Ralph traveled all over the United States doing luncheon seminars and promoting his book.

At a luncheon seminar in a small midwestern town with approximately 100 persons attending, Ralph asked the group questions about ghosts. The first question asked to the group was "How many of you have ever dreamed you saw a ghost"? Just about everyone present raised their hand. Next question; "How many of you have ever dreamed you talked to a ghost and the ghost answered"? About 75 people raised their hand. Next question, "How many of you have ever actually seen a ghost"? Only 15 people raised their hand. The last question Ralph always asks at each seminar but he has never had anyone raise their hand, "How many of you present today have had a sexual experience with a ghost"? Ralph looks over the group to see if anyone has a hand raised. Way back in the last row an elderly gentleman is frantically waving his hand. "Sir, can you come forward to the podium" Ralph asks. The elderly gentleman makes his way up the aisle and onto the stage, Ralph hands him the microphone and says "Please tell the people present today about your sexual experience with a ghost". The elderly gentleman replied "ghost, I'm sorry I thought you said goat"!

"I don't think the Inspector has seen it yet."

## RATE SCHEDULE

ANSWERS..................................$1.00
ANSWERS WHICH
REQUIRE THOUGHT ....................$2.00
CORRECT ANSWERS ..................$4.00

DUMB LOOKS ARE STILL FREE ............

## Question?

What is 10 - 9 - 8 - 7 - 6?
(see answer section)

Don't be afraid to ask dumb questions,
they're easier to handle than dumb mistakes.

Ford used to have a better idea;
now they don't have a clue.

Here's to our wives and
sweethearts - may they
never meet.

**NEVER ENGAGE IN A BATTLE OF WITS WITH AN UNARMED PERSON.**

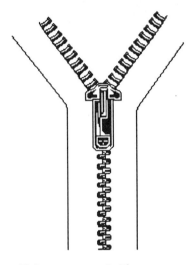

**Flies spread disease -
keep yours zipped.**

## HEAVY THOUGHTS:

**If you don't go to other people's funerals, they won't go to yours.**

QUESTION?

What word has twelve
letters and means to
have and to hold?

See answer section.

A friend is a person that
know's all about you,
but loves you anyway.

IF IT HAS BREASTS OR BRAKES,
YOU'RE GONNA HAVE PROBLEMS
WITH IT!

## HEAVY THOUGHTS:

I was born in New Zealand because my mother wanted me to be near her.

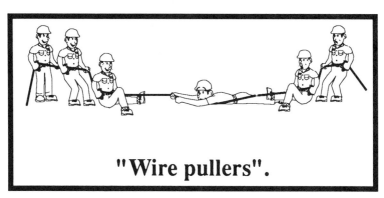

"Wire pullers".

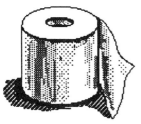

Today you can go to a gas station and find the cash register open and the rest rooms locked. They must think toilet paper is worth more than money.

I SHALL NEVER QUENCH MY THIRST FOR EDUCATION.

The city slicker asked the country boy if he had change for an $18 bill. The country boy replied "do you want two- 9's or six - 3's"?

MILITARY TIME

ARMY PERSONNEL it's 4 PM

NAVY PERSONNEL it's 1600

and for you big tough MARINES, the little hand is on four and the big hand is on twelve.

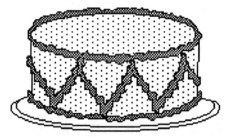

Failing an exam is like baking a cake with all the best ingredients and having someone sit on it.

You can put a suit on a monkey,
but you still got a monkey.

A tip from Tri-County Realty:

GET A LOT WHILE YOU'RE YOUNG!

HEAVY THOUGHTS:

NOW IS NOW.

**She had freckles on her, butt, she was pretty.**

The old farmer went to the eye doctor for an examination.
When completing the exam the doctor asked the farmer,
"have you ever had a cataract before"?
The old farmer answered "no, but I had a 55 Ford once"!

**Great moments in science: Einstein discovers that time is actually money.**

**GEORGE BUSH HAS AGREED
TO BE THE FIRST
ARTIFICIAL HEART DONOR.**

Money can't buy everything.
That's why there are credit cards.

Opportunities are usually disguised by hard
work, so most people don't recognize them.

The dictionary is the only place
where success comes before work.

Skiing combines outdoor fun with knocking down
trees with your face.

 The reason so many people fly off the handle is that they have a screw loose.

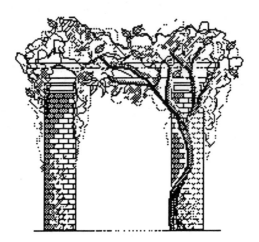

The doctor can bury his mistakes but an architect can only advise his client to plant vines.

**Don't be in a hurry to take down the shutters until there is something in the window.**

**We cannot direct the wind but we can adjust the sails.**

**Let a smile be your umbrella, because you're going to get soaked anyway.**

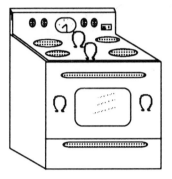

Ohm, Ohm on the range.

Which one of them is Delta Highleg?

> Pray for what you want,
> but work for the things you need.

When they asked George Washington for his ID,
he reached in his pocket and took out a quarter.

A well-balanced diet is a
pizza in each hand.

> It's easier to go down hill than up,
> but the view is better from the top.

**IMPROVE YOUR IMAGE,
BE SEEN WITH AN
ELECTRICIAN!**

He who hesitates is not only lost, but miles from the next exit.

 In the newspaper people are dying in alphabetical order.

Not all books are bound to do well.

**HEAVY THOUGHTS:**

I believe that people would be alive today if there were a death penalty.

After a year of therapy, my psychiatrist said to me, "Maybe life isn't for everyone."

Has the snake come through yet?

Answer to Code book question.

There ain't no answer.
There ain't going to be any answer.
There never has been an answer.
That's the answer.

When a man brings his wife flowers for no reason - there's a reason.

An expert is someone who brings confusion to simplicity.

Hear no evil, speak no evil, see no evil, and you'll never be an electrician.

If I had known that my son was going to be an inspector, I would have taught him to read and write.

| S | M | T | W | T | F | S |
|---|---|---|---|---|---|---|
| 1 | 2 | 3 | 4 | 5 | 6 | 7 |
| 8 | 9 | 10 | 11 | 12 | 13 | 14 |
| 15 | 16 | 17 | 18 | 19 | 20 | 21 |
| 22 | 23 | 24 | 25 | 26 | 27 | 28 |
| 29 | 30 | 31 | | | | |

**Why is there so much month
left at the end of the money?**

**Dynamite if you ask her.**

 **Today, the only thing that is
free of charge is a day-old
battery.**

**I don't drink that much, I spill some of it.**

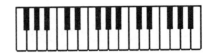

**When his wife put in her new set of false teeth she looked like she had a whole mouth full of piano keys.**

## Think twice; do once.

Use the talents you possess; for the woods would be very silent if no birds sang except the best.

**HEAVY THOUGHTS:**

If I had more time, I would write a shorter book.

QUESTION?

What part of a
woman's body is
called her "now"?

See answer section.

Imagination is more important than knowledge.

No matter how wealthy you become, how famous
or powerful, when you die the size of the funeral
will still pretty much depend on the weather.

> Sometimes all it takes to solve our problems is a fresh morning.

There ain't no rules around here!
We're trying to accomplish something!

> He was so sick that I went and had my good suit pressed.

I like trees because they seem more resigned to
the way they have to live than other things do.

My grandmother's brain was dead, but her heart was still beating. It was the first time we ever had a Republican in the family.

Many men die at twenty-five and aren't buried until they are seventy-five.

Arguing with an inspector is like wrestling with a pig in the mud. After a while you realize the pig enjoys it!

Someone once asked Einstein how many feet are in a mile. "I don't know", Einstein is reported as saying. "Why should I fill my head with things like that when I could look them up in any reference book in two minutes?"

I don't drink anymore, but I don't drink any less!

HEAVY THOUGHTS:

I really didn't say everything I said.

QUESTION?

What part of a
woman's body is
called her "yet"?

See answer section.

"DRAIN SURGEON"

25 HOUR SERVICE

The plumber can put his plumbing license
in the windshield, that way he can qualify
for handicapped parking.

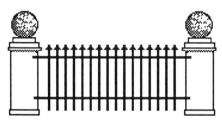

The cemeteries are filled with people who thought
the world couldn't get along without them.

The higher a monkey climbs,
the more you see of its behind.

**THERE ARE MORE HORSE'S ASSES THAN HORSES.**

The trouble with using experience as a guide is that the exam often comes first and then Code Electrical Classes.

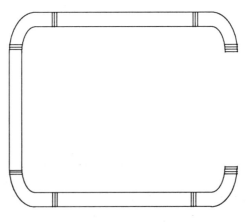

An open circuit.

The trouble with eating Italian food is that six or seven days later you're hungry again.

There are three reasons why lawyers are replacing rats as laboratory research animals. One is that they're plentiful, another is that lab assistants don't get attached to them, and the third is that there are some things rats just won't do.

Those who say it can't be done are usually interrupted by others doing it.

He's so tight that when he opens his wallet, George Washington has to shield his eyes from the light.

**HEAVY THOUGHTS:**

That restaurant is so crowded nobody goes there anymore.

 The mind is like a TV: When it goes blank, it's a good idea to turn off the sound.

Learn to eat problems for breakfast.

TODAY'S SPECIAL
**FROG
LEGS**

"Galvani must still be in the kitchen!"

 When the inspector gave me his two cents worth, he was overcharging.

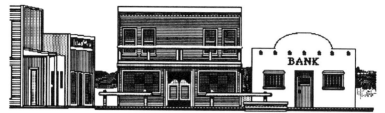

A student in class was from a small western town. When asked where it was located the reply was, "drive to the end of the earth, and then it's 3 more hours.

I quit drinking! About 3am this morning.

Fall is my favorite season in LA, watching the birds change color and fall from the trees.

My parents didn't want to move to Florida, but they retired, and it was the law.

A sign of old age is when you stop buying green bananas and long playing records.

If you drink, don't drive. Don't even putt.

**WHAT PART OF NO
DON'T YOU
UNDERSTAND?**

While walking through a shopping mall I was stopped and asked to answer some survey questions pertaining to the upcoming Presidential election.

The person asked me if I was a Democrat or a Republican. I answered "Democrat".

They asked "why did you choose the Democratic party"? I said my mother is a Democrat. They said "that doesn't mean you have to be a Democrat just because your mother is a Democrat". "What if your mother had been a horse thief"?

"Then I would of been a Republican" I answered!

**We were so poor... when burglars broke into our house, all they got was practice.**

**Marriage is a great institution, but I'm not ready for an institution.**

**HEAVY THOUGHTS:**

**I bought some batteries, but they weren't included.**

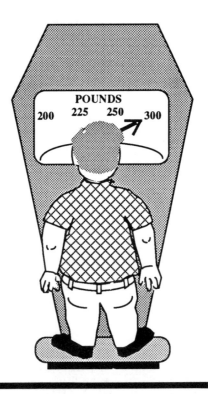

The man who doesn't read Tom Henry's books has no advantage over the 70 million people who can't read.

**Fortune Card**

**You're so fat your birthday covers 3 days!**

**Reading the Code book is kind of like staring at a cow for forty minutes.**

**Studying the Code book is the most fun you can have without smiling.**

**The electrician can't speak his mind, but the inspector can. He has nothing to lose.**

The most unexpected injury most people suffer nowadays is being struck by an idea.

You never fail until you stop trying.

YOU CANNOT FAIL UNTIL
YOU'VE BEEN A SUCCESS ONCE.

IF IT AIN'T BROKE
DON'T FIX IT!

Does the name Alexander Graham ring a bell?

**What's the difference between a pipefitter and a plumber?**

(see answer section)

Retirement is when you finally have the time to sink your teeth into something fun, but you don't have any teeth left.

**HEAVY THOUGHTS:**

The sooner you fall behind, the more time you will have to catch up.

"Ralph, get yours straightened up!"

EXPERIENCE ......
IS SIMPLY THE NAME WE
GIVE OUR MISTAKES.

The difference between genius and
stupidity is that genius has its limits.

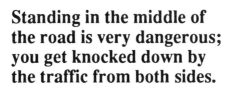

Standing in the middle of
the road is very dangerous;
you get knocked down by
the traffic from both sides.

Just remember, when you're over the hill,
you begin to pick up speed.

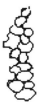

The only difference between a
stumbling block and a stepping
stone is the way you use it.

IF YOUR SHIP DOESN'T COME IN,
SWIM OUT TO IT.

133

I figured out I was an unwanted child when
I saw my bath toys; a radio and toaster.

## LOVE IS FREE,
## PENICILLIN COSTS.

The reason Las Vegas is so
crowded is that no one has any
money left to buy a bus ticket.

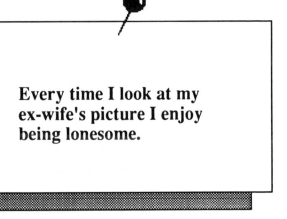

Every time I look at my
ex-wife's picture I enjoy
being lonesome.

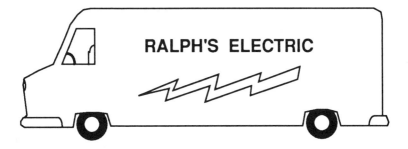

RALPH'S ELECTRIC

**I locked my keys in the truck and I had to break the window to get my helper out.**

**Those supplies necessary for yesterday's job must be ordered no later than noon tomorrow.**

If I ever needed a brain transplant, I'd choose a supervisor because I'd want a brain that had never been used.

With test taking, it's not what we don't know that hurts, it's what we know that ain't so.

Experience teaches you to recognize a mistake when you've made it again.

He's alive but unconscious, he must be an engineer.

## The Inspector's Dog

Four workers were discussing how smart their dogs were. The first was an engineer, who said his dog could do math with calculations. His dog was named "T-Square". He told him to get some paper and draw a square, a circle and a triangle, which the dog did with no sweat.

The electrician said he thought his dog was better. His dog was named "Slide Rule". He told him to fetch a dozen cookies, bring them back and divide them into piles of three, which he did with no problem.

The plumber said that was good, but he said his dog was better. His dog was named "Measure". He told his dog to get a quart of milk and pour seven ounces into a ten-ounce glass. The dog did with no problem.

All three men agreed this was very good and their dogs were equally smart.

They all turned to the inspector and said, "what can your dog do?" The inspector called his dog whose name was "Coffee Break", and said, "show these fellows what you can do."

Coffee Break went over and ate the cookies, drank the milk, crapped on the paper, had sex with the other three dogs and claimed he injured his back while doing so, filed a grievance for unsafe working conditions, applied for Workman's Compensation and left for home on sick leave.

137

**Horsepower was a wonderful thing when only horses had it.**

Feb 31

$9.00

**I'm going to move so far away that they'll have to put a nine dollar stamp on a post card to reach me.**

HEAVY THOUGHTS:

When trying to solve a problem, it always helps if you know the answer.

 Churches welcome all denominations, but most prefer tens and twentys.

Electrical Engineer

B.S.
M.S.
P.H.D.

The B.S. is what you thought it was, the M.S. is more of the same, the P.H.D., piled higher and deeper.

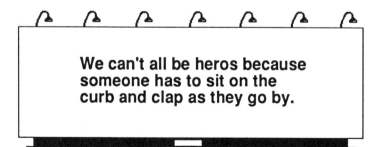 We can't all be heros because someone has to sit on the curb and clap as they go by.

THE MOST POWERFUL NATION ON EARTH IS DETERMINATION.

## QUESTION?

From what number can you take away half and leave nothing?

See answer section.

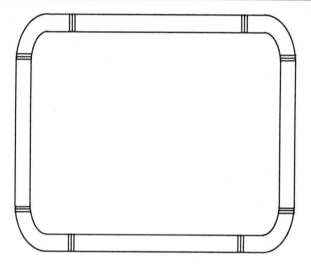

A closed circuit.

Always get married early in the morning. That way, if it doesn't work out, you haven't wasted a whole day.

140

HAZARDOUS MATERIALS INFORMATION
# MATERIAL SAFETY DATA SHEET

## WOMAN - A CHEMICAL ANALYSIS

**ELEMENT:** Woman
**SYMBOL:** $WO^2$
**DISCOVERER:** Adam
**ATOMIC MASS:** Accepted at 118 lbs., but known to vary from 100 to 550 pounds.
**OCCURENCE:** Copious quantities in all urban areas.

## PHYSICAL PROPERTIES:

1. Surface usually covered with a painted film.
2. Boils at nothing, freezes without reason.
3. Melts if given special treatment.
4. Bitter if incorrectly used.
5. Found in various states, ranging from virgin metal to common ore.
6. Yields to pressure applied to correct points.

## CHEMICAL PROPERTIES:

1. Has a great affinity for Gold, Silver, Platinum and precious stones.
2. Absorbs great quantities of expensive substances.
3. May explode spontaneously without prior warning for no reason.
4. Insoluble in liquids, but activity greatly increased by alcohol.
5. Most powerful money-reducing agent known to man.

## COMMON USES:

1. Highly ornamental, especially in sports cars.
2. Can be a great aid to relaxation.

## TESTS:

1. Pure specimen turns rosy pink when discovered in the natural state.
2. Turns green when placed beside a better specimen.

## HAZARDS:

1. Highly dangerous except in experienced hands.
2. Illegal to possess more than one.

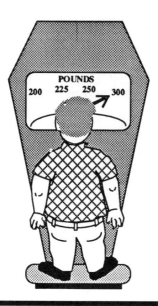

POUNDS

200    225    250        300

**Fortune Card**

For your weight to be
proportional to your height
you need to be 37 feet tall.

---

**People forget how fast you did a job,
but they remember how well you did it.**

---

**QUESTION?**

**What's an inspector
do on a slow day?**

**See answer section.**

By working faithfully
eight hours a day you
may eventually get to be
a boss and work twelve
hours a day.

BIG DEAL!

I'm used
to dust.

I'm so poor, I can't even pay attention.

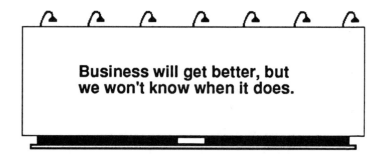

Business will get better, but
we won't know when it does.

WALK
DON'T WALK

Come and pick me up, I'm in a phone booth
at the corner of Walk and Don't Walk.

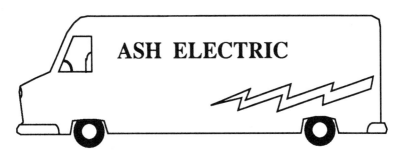

**It's a new company in town and they are underbidding everyone.**

$$$$

Supply counter

Will call

MasterCard

*VISA*

How much does a GFCI 20 amp breaker cost? $16 replied the counter salesman. The electrician stated "I can buy one across the street for only $12". "Why don't you go across the street and buy one" was the counterman's reply. "They don't have any" said the electrician. The counter man said "when we don't have any they are only $8."

When the electrician's wife turned 40 years old he decided he ought to trade her in for two 20 year olds.
But then he found out he wasn't wired for 220!

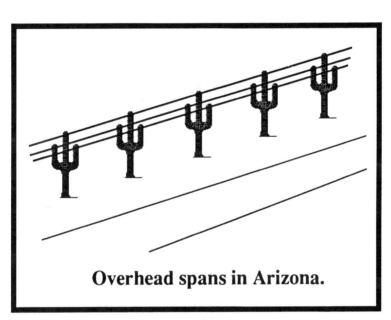

Overhead spans in Arizona.

It doesn't matter if you're on the right track, you'll still get run over if you don't keep moving.

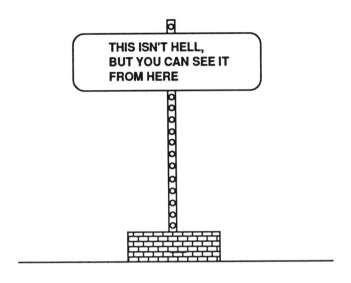

City limits.

A practical cookbook is one that has a blank page in the back - where you can list the numbers of the nearest delicatessen.

ANY FOOL CAN CRITICIZE,
CONDEMN AND COMPLAIN -
AND MOST DO.

NEW YORK    TOKYO    CAIRO

HONG KONG    LONDON    FORT WAYNE,
INDIANA

While doing a class in Indianapolis which started at 8am,
one student arrived at 8:30am. I mentioned to him he was
late and his reply was. "Hey, in Ft. Wayne there's a
half-hour difference in time".

A bank is a place where
they lend you an umbrella
in nice weather and ask
for it back when it begins
to rain.

148

"I just plugged it in to see if you fixed it."

## QUESTION?

What six-letter word can you take one letter away from and still leave twelve?

See answer section.

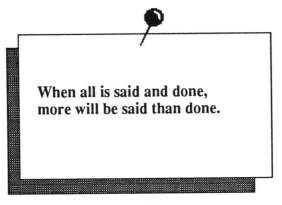

When all is said and done,
more will be said than done.

## Energizing A Relay!

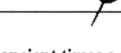

In ancient times a woman was considered old at the age of forty. Today a woman of that age is only twenty-nine.

An army of sheep led by a lion would defeat an army of lions led by a sheep.

# Understanding the Technology!

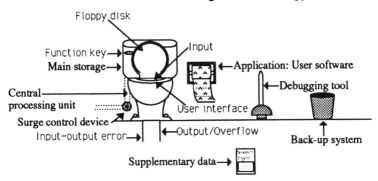

He was outstanding in school,
out standing in the hall.

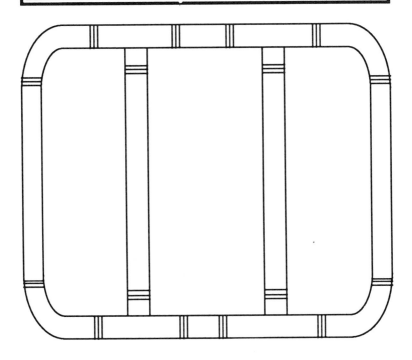

**A parallel circuit.**

**DEFINITIONS:**

**RECESSION** - A period in which you tighten up your belt.

**DEPRESSION** - You have no belt to tighten up.

**PANIC** - You have no pants to hold up.

**FINESSE:**
Is when you can tell someone to go to hell and they look forward to the trip.

If men could see the epitaphs their friends write they would believe they had gotten into the wrong grave.

152

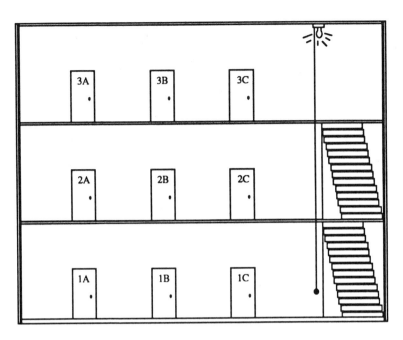

## THE FIRST 3-WAY SWITCH

BUYING INSURANCE IS WHAT
KEEPS PEOPLE POOR SO THEY
CAN DIE RICH.

New Years Resolution:

I'm going to live within my income this year
even if I have to borrow money to do it!

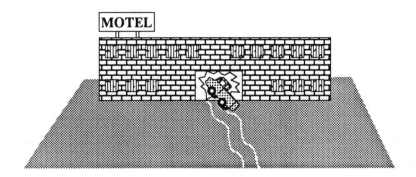

A motel in a small town caught fire one morning and the guests ran from the building to the parking lot watching the motel burn while awaiting the local volunteer fire department to arrive. At the same time an electrical service truck came speeding down the hill and drove straight into the lobby of the motel. The electrician jumped out of the truck and took off his jacket and beat the flames from the fire out.

The volunteer fire department arrived only to find the motel guests standing in the parking lot cheering the lone electrician for his bravery.

The town mayor applauded the electrician for his heroism. After talking with motel management they decided to award the electrician $500 for his act of bravery.

As the mayor handed the electrician the $500 he asked him how he planned to spend the money?

The electrician replied "the first thing I'm gonna do is get the brakes fixed on that truck"!

**Any wire cut to length will be too short.**

**His mother should have thrown him away and kept the stork.**

**"Motors must run on smoke, because when you let all the smoke out, it quits running!"**

**HALF OF ANALYSIS IS ANAL.**

An alcoholic is a person who drinks more than his own doctor.

**The hour of departure has arrived and we must go our ways; I die, and you to live. Which is better? Only God knows.**

**O Lord, help me to be pure, but not yet.**

**HEAVY THOUGHTS:**

Most born executives are people with a parent who started the business.

Always remember, for every "10" there are ten 1's.

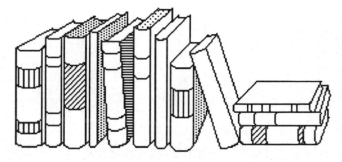

**Eighty percent of the final exam will be based on the one book you didn't read.**

It's a good thing that when God created the rainbow He didn't consult a decorator or He would still be picking colors.

If you've got to kick the bucket, it's best to die with your boots on.

Everyone wants to go to Heaven, but nobody wants to die.

**IF YOU DON'T CARE WHERE YOU ARE, YOU AIN'T LOST.**

**To err is human, but to really foul things up requires an engineer.**

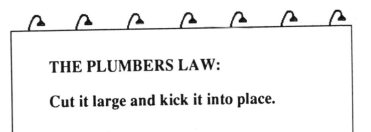

THE PLUMBERS LAW:

Cut it large and kick it into place.

Question?

What is the only animal you eat before born and after they are dead?

## The big dark sucker set.

The difference between a
taxidermist and a tax collector
is the taxidermist takes only
your skin.

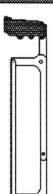

## I've cut it three times,
## and it's still too short.

My parents were too poor to have children,
so the neighbors had me.

 I have a photographic mind,
I just have trouble developing
the film.

Boss, I remembered you saying you like
a doughnut with your tea at break time!

**Do you have any current books?**
**Yes, a brand new one on lightning.**

IT'S OKAY TO LAUGH IN
THE BEDROOM SO LONG
AS YOU DON'T POINT.

**The new inspector is tougher**
**than a 50¢ steak.**

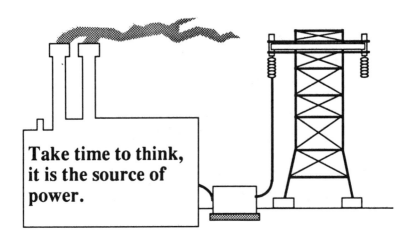

Take time to think,
it is the source of
power.

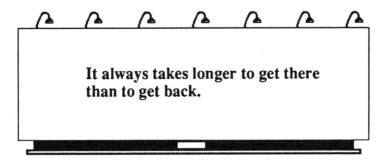

It always takes longer to get there
than to get back.

**HEAVY THOUGHTS:**

Things equal to nothing
else are equal to each
other.

**Take time to laugh, it is the Music of the Soul.**

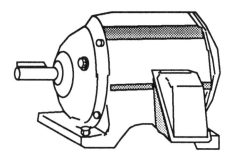

**A motor will rotate in the wrong direction.**

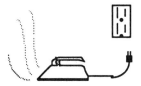

**It always works better if you plug it in.**

**HEAVY THOUGHTS:**

You cannot successfully determine beforehand which side of the bread to butter.

Take time to read. It is the Fountain of Wisdom.

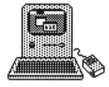

Computer programs advance so quickly that if your computer is over two years old about the only use it has now, is it can be used for a night light.

Everyone wants to be noticed, but no one wants to be stared at.

**HEAVY THOUGHTS:**

Kirchhoff's Law was not discovered by Kirchhoff, but by another man with the same name.

"What made you give up your last job as an electrician?"

**IF IT JAMS - FORCE IT.
IF IT BREAKS, IT NEEDED
REPLACING ANYWAY.**

All those Doctor certificates on the wall can be
awarded by making C's and D's. I want the
Doctor working on me to make all A's!

...oh, no!!!

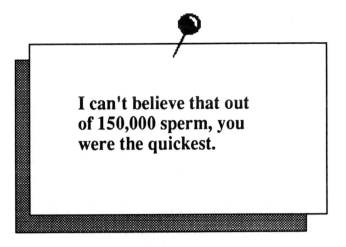

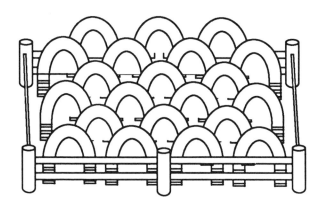

**A magnetic field.**

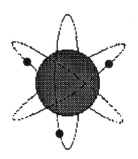

Electricity comes from electrons and protons.

If the electrician becomes charged too often the formula is:

**ELECTRONS + PROTONS = ONE MORON!**

Question?

What is black when clean and white when dirty?

Other than for that brief
moment, Mrs. Lincoln,
how did you like the play?

My twin sister was my "womb mate".

**HEAVY THOUGHTS:**

Anyone who is popular
is bound to be disliked.

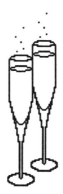

When making a toast the clinking of the glasses is to test your fourth sense, sound. The other three are sight, smell and taste.

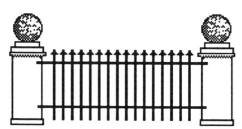

They say such nice things about people at their funerals that it makes me sad to realize that I'm going to miss mine by just a few days.

I was born at night, but I wasn't born last night!

**STUDY**

The more we study, the more we know.
The more we know, the more we forget.
The more we forget, the less we know.
The less we know, the less we forget.
The less we forget, the more we know.

So why study?

Experience may not be worth what
it costs, but we can't seem to get it
for any less.

Education is what a fellow
gets reading the fine print
and experience is what he
gets by not reading it.

# ELECTRICAL PERFORMANCE APPRAISAL

| PERFORMANCE FACTORS | ELECTRICIAN | HELPER | APPRENTICE | INSPECTOR | PLUMBER |
|---|---|---|---|---|---|
| QUALITY | Leaps tall buildings with a single bound. | Must take running start to leap over tall buildings. | Can leap over short buildings only. | Crashes into building when attempting to jump over it. | Cannot recognize buildings at all. |
| TIMELINESS | Is faster than a speeding bullet. | Is as fast as a speeding bullet. | Not quite as fast as a speeding bullet. | Would you believe slow. | Wounds self with bullet when attempting to shoot. |
| INITIATIVE | Is stronger than a locomotive. | Is stronger than a bull elephant. | Is stronger than a bull. | Shoots the bull. | Smells like a bull. |
| ADAPTABILITY | Walks on water consistently. | Walks on water in emergencies. | Washes with water. | Drinks water. | Passes water in emergencies. |
| COMMUNICATION | Talks with God. | Talks with the angels. | Talks to himself. | Argues with himself. | Loses these arguments. |

## The big dark sucker

# CRACK

# KILLS

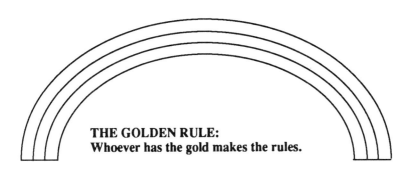

**THE GOLDEN RULE:**
Whoever has the gold makes the rules.

IF YOU DRINK LIKE A FISH,
DON'T DRIVE.
SWIM.

God has
always been
hard on the
poor.

175

**They are celebrating 3 years of happy marriage on their 14th wedding anniversary.**

**Everybody should believe in something -
I believe I'll have another drink.**

**There is nothing wrong with sex on tv, as long as you don't touch the high-voltage portion of the picture tube.**

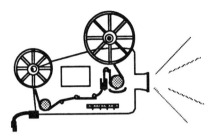

Movie theater business was so slow in a small midwestern town in the winter that when I called and asked what time the movie started, they said what time can you come down?

When I'm good, I'm really good.
And when I'm bad, I'm better.

No I don't jog, I want
to be sick when I die.

**An empty car stopped and an inspector got out.**

**Anybody can be good in the country.**

I'VE ONLY MET FOUR PERFECT
PEOPLE IN MY LIFE AND I
DIDN'T LIKE ANY OF THEM.

HEAVY THOUGHTS:

It is better to know
some of the questions
than all of the answers.

See if you can circle the 16 words related to electricity in the puzzle.

BATTERY       INSULATORS      FLOW       METAL
CHARGES      THUNDERSTORM    SPARK      CLOUD
POSITIVE      PARTICLE        STATIC      SHIELD
    CURRENT      LIGHTNING      VOLTS
             SOLAR ENERGY

| A | Y | C | L | A | T | E | M | D | U | O | L | C |
|---|---|---|---|---|---|---|---|---|---|---|---|---|
| M | R | D | I | P | U | Y | X | M | Z | A | I | T |
| R | E | V | G | O | V | N | O | S | L | T | K | P |
| O | T | E | H | W | F | R | G | H | A | I | J | A |
| T | T | C | T | P | O | S | I | T | I | V | E | R |
| S | A | H | N | T | L | A | S | P | A | R | K | T |
| R | B | A | I | P | E | L | F | T | G | H | D | I |
| E | N | R | N | B | S | H | I | E | L | D | I | C |
| D | M | G | G | S | O | R | C | L | K | O | J | L |
| N | T | E | U | V | W | O | L | F | H | T | V | E |
| U | O | S | O | L | A | R | E | N | E | R | G | Y |
| H | A | S | R | O | T | A | L | U | S | N | I | X |
| T | N | E | R | R | U | C | L | L | B | N | D | G |

(see answer section)

## "Load balancing"

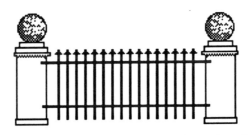

The fence around the cemetery is foolish, for those inside can't get out and those outside don't want to get in.

AS LONG AS THERE ARE
ELECTRICAL EXAMS,
THERE WILL BE PRAYER.

Lack of ambition is often mistaken for patience.

## THE SHORTEST DISTANCE BETWEEN TWO POINTS IS USUALLY UNDER REPAIR.

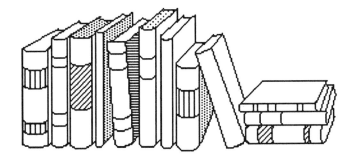

The exam is in one week and I don't have time to go through my books. What can I do?
Answer: Eat your books and let them go through you.

Plans examiner.

See if you can circle the 20 words related to electricity in the puzzle.

| BATTERY | DIRECT CURRENT | ATOM | LIGHT |
|---|---|---|---|
| CHARGES | ELECTRICITY | STATIC | PROTON |
| RHEOSTAT | ELECTROSCOPE | POWER | PLUG |
| NEUTRON | MORSE CODE | ELECTRON | FUSE |
| ENERGY | TELEGRAPH | SOCKET | CIRCUIT |

```
E  L  E  C  T  R  O  S  C  O  P  E  P
E  L  L  I  T  N  S  E  G  R  A  H  C
C  E  E  R  H  O  Y  R  E  T  T  A  B
N  L  S  C  U  T  M  O  O  R  A  S  H
O  I  E  U  T  O  C  M  D  E  T  T  A
R  G  E  I  F  R  S  L  E  C  S  E  R
T  H  R  T  I  P  I  C  T  Y  O  K  D
U  T  M  O  R  S  E  C  O  D  E  C  W
E  B  E  U  S  T  A  T  I  C  H  O  O
N  H  P  A  R  G  E  L  E  T  R  S  R
G  U  L  P  S  E  N  E  R  G  Y  U  S
E  L  E  C  T  R  O  N  R  E  W  O  P
T  N  E  R  R  U  C  T  C  E  R  I  D
```

**(see answer section)**

Ideas are like rabbits.
You get a couple and
learn how to handle
them, and pretty soon
you have a dozen.

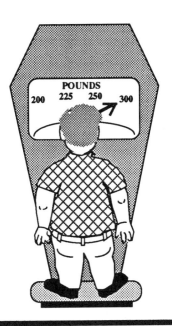

**Fortune Card**

You must look like a
bowling ball with feet!

If you are caught on a golf course during a storm and are afraid of lightning, hold up a 1-iron. Not even God can hit a 1-iron.

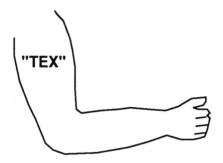

"TEX"

One electrician noticed a tatoo "TEX" on the other electricians's arm. "I guess you must be from Texas" he stated. "No, actually I'm from Louisiana, but I didn't want to be called Louise".

If the Republicans will stop telling lies about the Democrats, we will stop telling the truth about them.

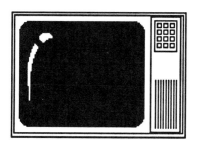

**If it weren't for the inventor of television, we'd still be eating frozen radio dinners.**

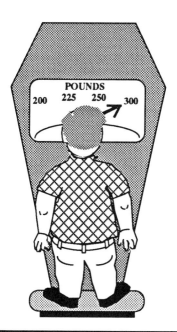

Fortune Card

It doesn't matter if you're short,
if you have money.
You can stand on your wallet.

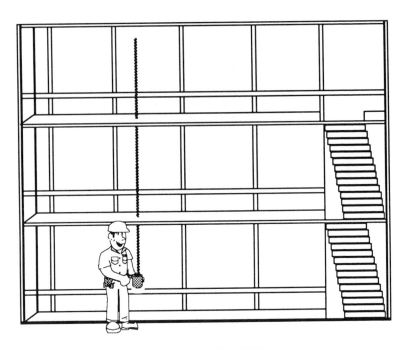

## THE BIG BIT!

**Grandma was slow,
but she was old.**

186

Nobody has ever bet enough on the winning horse.

The most fattening thing you can put on an ice cream sundae is a spoon.

It's okay to drink like a fish, as long as you drink what a fish drinks.

It's true when you die you can't take it with you, but nowadays you can't even afford to go.

I've put away the screwdrivers and wrenches,
but there's not enough room in the tool box for
the stripper!

The difference between a
"yankee" girl and a
"southern" girl is, a
yankee girl says "I love
you" and a southern girl
says "I love you all".

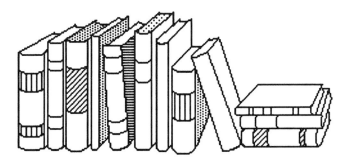

Anyone who eats three meals a day should understand why cookbooks outsell sex books three to one.

Why did you get a haircut on company time when you know its against company policy? "It grew on company time"! "Yes, but it didn't all grow on company time". "I didn't get it all cut off"!

Time flies like an arrow. Fruit flies like a banana.

**IN YOUR DREAMS .....**

Interpretation of the mysterious force of ELECTRICITY is influenced by details and action, but as a general guide if you dream of:

Turning electricity ON forecasts unexpected recognition for past efforts or favors.

Turning electricity OFF indicates depression or discouragement probably due to low vitality. A rest or vacation is suggested.

Short-circuiting indicates possible business reversal or property loss due to carelessness.

Being shocked by a live wire or static electricity signifies sudden surprising news.

A sudden power failure suggests waste of energy; reassess ambitions or consider a possible change.

To be aware of a live wire (as opposes to being shocked by it) warns of sudden opposition which will require careful diplomacy. Don't force issues.

A lit lamp signifies success.

An unlit lamp signifies disappointment.

Decorative lamps signify festive occasions.

Red lamp - WARNING.

Back to the basics; to dream of a kite: this is an obstacle dream whether you flew it yourself or saw others flying them, you can expect to achieve highest hopes if the kite flew easily and a happy omen is intensified if children are involved. However, if a string broke or kite was damaged or blew away, be prepared for a disappointment due to careless management of affairs.

Lightning - LUCK like a bolt from the blue will surely follow a dream of this electrical phenomenon of nature UNLESS rain and thunder also were within the dream. There still will be good luck but preceded by a period of anxiety.

Heat lightning indicates exciting social events will follow.

Lightning rod indicates possible interference in plans due to jealousy - be careful with all confidences.

Dream on - Dream on -

190

# ANSWER
# SECTION

# ANSWERS

**Page 18 - The answer is 9.**
100 divided by half is 100/50 = 2 plus 7 = 9

**Page 19 - The answer is 6.**
A person with average intelligence finds three.
If you found four you are above average.
If you found five you have a very strong mind.
If you found all **six** you are a genius!
• If you didn't find any you probably work as a plans examiner.
• If you found one you could hire on as a tree trimmer.
• If you found two you would skip 2 years plumbing school.

**Page 40 - The answer is because birds sit on the NEUTRAL!**

**Page 46 - The answers are : Are you dead? Are you asleep?**

**Page 56 - The answer is the one on the RIGHT.**

If the paper was put on the other way the pattern
on the paper would not be shown.

**Page 57 - The answer is a HUSBAND!**

**Page 71 - Electricity does not know how to CONDUCT
itself!**

Page 99 -   The answer is BO DEREK getting older.
            Bo in her younger days was a 10!

Page 102 -  The answer is CONSTIPATION.

Page 117 -   I don't know but I heard this song on the
            radio "I wonder who's kissing her <u>NOW</u>."

Page 121 -  I don't know. But I read in the newspaper
            where a lady had been shot and they haven't
            gotten the bullet out of her <u>YET</u>.

Page 131 -  A plumber doesn't chew his fingernails.

Page 135 -  The letter "M".

Page 140 -  The number is **8**.

take away and it leaves

Page 142 -  Watches paint dry.

Page 149 -    **The answer is DOZENS.**


Page 160 -    **A chicken.**


Page 169 -    **A blackboard.**


The answers to pages 179 and 182 are on the next pages.

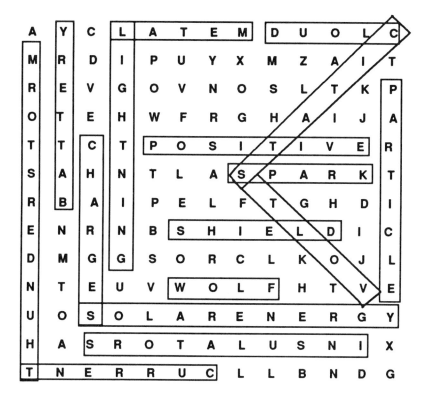

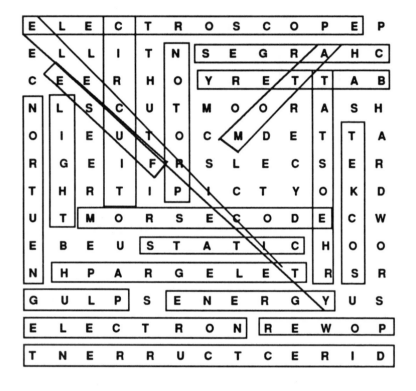

# *Tom Henry's* CODE ELECTRICAL CLASSES & BOOKSTORE

6832 Hanging Moss Road  Orlando, Florida 32807
1-800-642-2633

Calls are taken Monday through Friday 8am to 6pm Eastern time

Bill Fuson - Shipping Manager
Mary  Gray - Graphic Arts
Tim Henry - Vice President
and Manager of Operations

A complete line of electrical
books are available at the
bookstore.

## ELECTRICAL SEMINARS TAUGHT IN 20 STATES

Tom Henry and son Tim Henry Principal Instructors